I AM INCAPABLE (AND THAT'S OKAY)

100+ Disappointing Affirmations for Embracing the Bare Minimum

S. B. COLLECTIVE

ISBN: 978-1-7645150-0-9 (Paperback)
ISBN: 978-1-7645150-1-6 (Hardcover)

This publication includes images generated using Artificial Intelligence (AI).

Book Design by HMDPublishing.com

For the high-functioning avoidant, the elite-level postponer,
and anyone currently looking for a reason to stop trying.

Your era has arrived.
(Go forth and achieve nothing, elegantly.)

ABANDON ALL HOPE (OF BEING INSPIRED)

You've clearly reached a point of desperation. Either you bought this for yourself because your vision board caught fire, or someone who knows you very well decided you needed a reality check. Either way, congratulations: You've finally failed.

This isn't a guide to success. It's a permission slip to stop trying. While other books promise to help you "unlock your potential," we are here to help you change the locks and pretend you aren't home.

Think of these pages as the cynical twin of every self-help book you've ever bought and never finished. We don't do "positive vibes" here. This is just a curated collection of 100+ artistic anti-affirmations celebrating the beauty of burnout and the absolute relief of the bare minimum.

Don't look for a "call to action." The only action we recommend is closing this book and acknowledging that the stars are millions of miles away. They don't care about your career goals.

Enjoy the descent. It's much easier than climbing.

CONGRATULATIONS.
YOU EXIST.
THAT'S ENOUGH
DISAPPOINTMENT
FOR ONE DAY.

EVERYTHING WILL BE FINE. IS WHAT I'D SAY IF YOU WEREN'T A JOKE.

YOU'RE
CONSISTENT... AT
DISAPPOINTING
EVERYONE.

FAILURE ISN'T AN OPTION. YOU BOUGHT THE LIFETIME SUBSCRIPTION.
APPROVED
LIFETIME

YOU'RE
LIVING PROOF
PARTICIPATION
TROPHIES WERE A
MISTAKE.

AMBITION FEARS YOU. KEEP SCROLLING.
AMBITION

YOU'RE
UNFORGETTABLE...
IN ALL THE
WRONG WAYS.

YOUR BED LOVES YOU MORE THAN ANYONE EVER COULD. RESPECT IT.

MOTIVATION EXISTS. YOU, ON THE OTHER HAND... NOT SO MUCH.

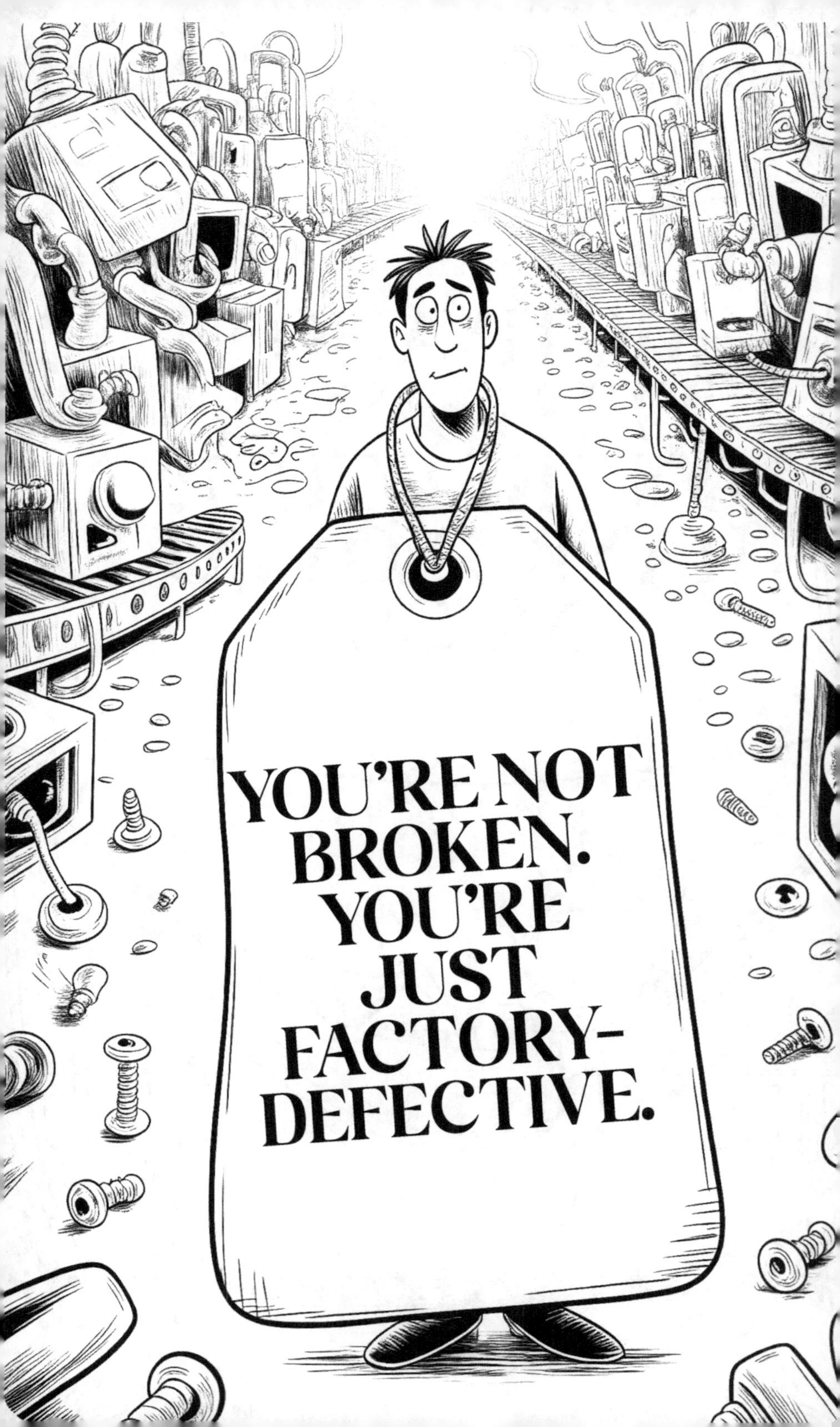
YOU'RE NOT
BROKEN.
YOU'RE
JUST
FACTORY-
DEFECTIVE.

HUMOR
>
PRODUCTIVITY.
YOU FAIL
AT BOTH,
BEAUTIFULLY.

YOU'RE EMOTIONALLY UNAVAILABLE... EVEN TO YOURSELF.

PRODUCTIVITY
CALLED.
YOU
IGNORED
IT. GOOD
CHOICE.

MISTAKES
ARE
PERMANENT.
YOU, FOR
EXAMPLE.

SOCIAL SKILLS CALLED. YOU WERE TOO UGLY TO ANSWER.

YOU'RE
UNIQUE.
LIKE EVERYONE
ELSE WHO
FAILED.

GOALS
HATE YOU.
GOALS ALWAYS
HATE YOU.

OVERTHINKING
IS YOUR
CARDIO.
GOLD MEDAL
GUARANTEED.

YOU'RE NOT
FAILING.
YOU'RE
JUST VERY
CONSISTENT.

CREATIVITY
GHOSTED
YOU.
PERMANENTLY.

YOU'RE
THE REASON
"TRY AGAIN"
BUTTONS
EXIST.

PERFECTION
IS FOR LOSERS.
LUCKY YOU'RE
A LOSER.

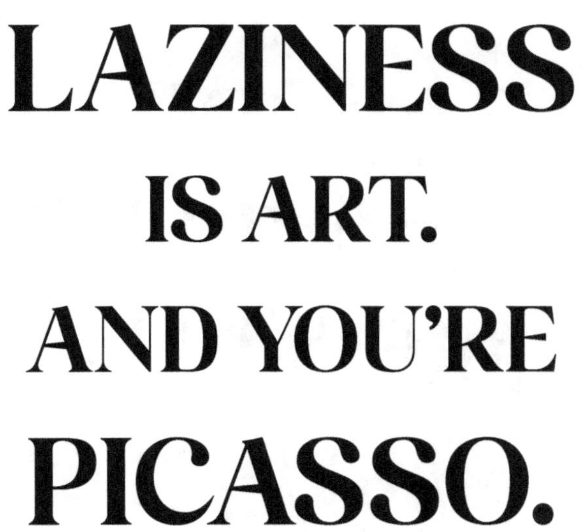
LAZINESS
IS ART.
AND YOU'RE
PICASSO.

YOU'RE
UNFORGETTABLE.
LIKE A TYPO
IN AN
IMPORTANT
EMAIL.

OVERCOMMITMENT?
YOU'RE
NATURALLY AN
UNDERACHIEVER.

YOU'RE NOT
UNLUCKY.
YOU'RE JUST
TERRIBLE
AT LIFE.

YOUR
INNER
CRITIC
DESERVES
A STANDING
OVATION.
TAKE A BOW.

YOUR DIET PLAN FAILED. JUST LIKE YOU DID.

YOU'RE
THE
PLOT
TWIST
NO ONE
ASKED
FOR.

EXERCISE FEARS YOU.
GRAVITY FORGIVES YOU.

YOU'RE
THE
REASON
MIRRORS
NEED
THERAPY.

HOPES AND
DREAMS
MOCK YOU
DAILY.

SELF-
IMPROVEMENT
IS A MYTH.
YOU'RE
LIVING PROOF.

SUCCESS
AVOIDS YOU.
YOU DON'T BLAME IT.

YOU'RE THE
REASON
FAILURE
GOT PROMOTED.

YOUR
COMFORT
ZONE
IS A
KINGDOM.
STAY THERE.

ADULT
CONVERSATIONS
TERRIFY YOU.
STICK TO
MEMES.

YOU'RE A
ROLE MODEL
... FOR WHAT
NOT TO DO.

DEADLINES
FEAR YOU.
YOU FEAR
THEM MORE.

YOU'RE
THE MAIN
CHARACTER...
IN A TRAGEDY.

MISTAKES
BUILD
CHARACTER.
YOU'RE A
SKYSCRAPER.

YOUR PLANTS
SURVIVE
DESPITE YOU.
BRAVE LITTLE
SOLDIERS...

LIFE IS
MESSY.
YOU FIT IN
PERFECTLY.
UNLIKE
YOUR JEANS.

IGNORANCE
ISN'T BLISS.
IT'S YOUR
LIFESTYLE.

YOU'LL
FORGET
THIS
AFFIRMATION.
CLASSIC.

SLEEP IN.
THE WORLD
SURVIVED
WORSE
WITHOUT YOU.
11 12 1
10 2
9 3
8 4
7 6 5

YOU'RE A
LIMITED
EDITION...
DISAPPOINTMENT.

MOTIVATION
DIED
WAITING
FOR YOU.

YOU'RE ALWAYS
RIGHT.
IN YOUR OWN
DELUSIONS.

OVERCOMMITMENT?
YOU ONLY
COMMIT
TO BAD
DECISIONS...
LIKE THIS
BOOK.

MOTIVATION
IS FLEETING.
UNLIKE YOUR
WEIGHT.

CONFIDENCE?
FAKE IT.
YOU'RE GOOD AT LYING ANYWAY.

DREAMS
ARE FREE.
PERFECT,
BECAUSE
YOU'RE BROKE.

REWARD
EFFORT
HARD WORK
PAYS OFF.
JUST NOT
FOR YOU.

YOU'RE NOT LAZY. YOU'RE ENERGY-EFFICIENT.

FAILURE
ISN'T FOLLOWING YOU.
YOU SPRINT
TOWARD IT.

YOU'RE NOT
LOST.
YOU'RE
DIRECTIONALLY
CHALLENGED.

DISCIPLINE
LEFT
THE
CHAT.

YOU'RE LIVING

PROOF THAT

THE UNIVERSE

HAS A SENSE OF HUMOR.

YOUR EXISTENCE LOWERS PROPERTY VALUES.
FOR SALE

YOU HAD POTENTIAL ONCE.
THEN YOU LOOKED IN THE MIRROR.

CONFIDENCE
IS QUIET.
YOUR
INSECURITY
IS SCREAMING.

YOUR
POTENTIAL
TOOK A
WRONG TURN...
AT BIRTH.

YOU
DREAM
BIG.
THEN HIT
SNOOZE.

MULTITASKING?
YOU CAN'T
EVEN
SINGLE-TASK.

YOU'RE A
LEGEND.
IN MISSED
OPPORTUNITIES.

YOU
COULD
WIN
AT LIFE.
IF THERE
WERE A
PARTICIPATION
PRIZE.

MEDIOCRITY LOOKS GOOD ON YOU.

STILL UGLY THOUGH.

YOU'RE
PROOF
EVOLUTION
CAN TAKE A
DAY OFF.

YOU WERE
BORN TO
STAND OUT.
IN A
CROWD OF
FAILURES.

YOUR
MOTIVATION
QUIT.
ON ITS
FIRST DAY.

SUCCESS AVOIDS YOU. AND SO SHOULD EVERYONE ELSE.

YOU'RE
INSPIRATIONAL...
TO PEOPLE
DOING BETTER
THAN YOU.

YOU GIVE
110%...
OF EXCUSES.

YOU'RE
THE WI-FI
OF LIFE.
ALWAYS
DROPPING
OUT.

YOU COULD TRIP... OVER A CORDLESS PHONE.

YOU'RE A
VIP.
VERY
INCOMPETENT
PERSON.

YOU TRIED
YOUR BEST.
THAT WAS
THE
PROBLEM.

BEFORE
AFTER
YOU'RE THE
"BEFORE"
PICTURE.
FOREVER.

EVERY DAY'S A FRESH START... TO FAIL AGAIN.

YOU INSPIRE NOTHING... EXCEPT REGRET.

YOU'RE A
MASTERPIECE...
OF
INCOMPETENCE.

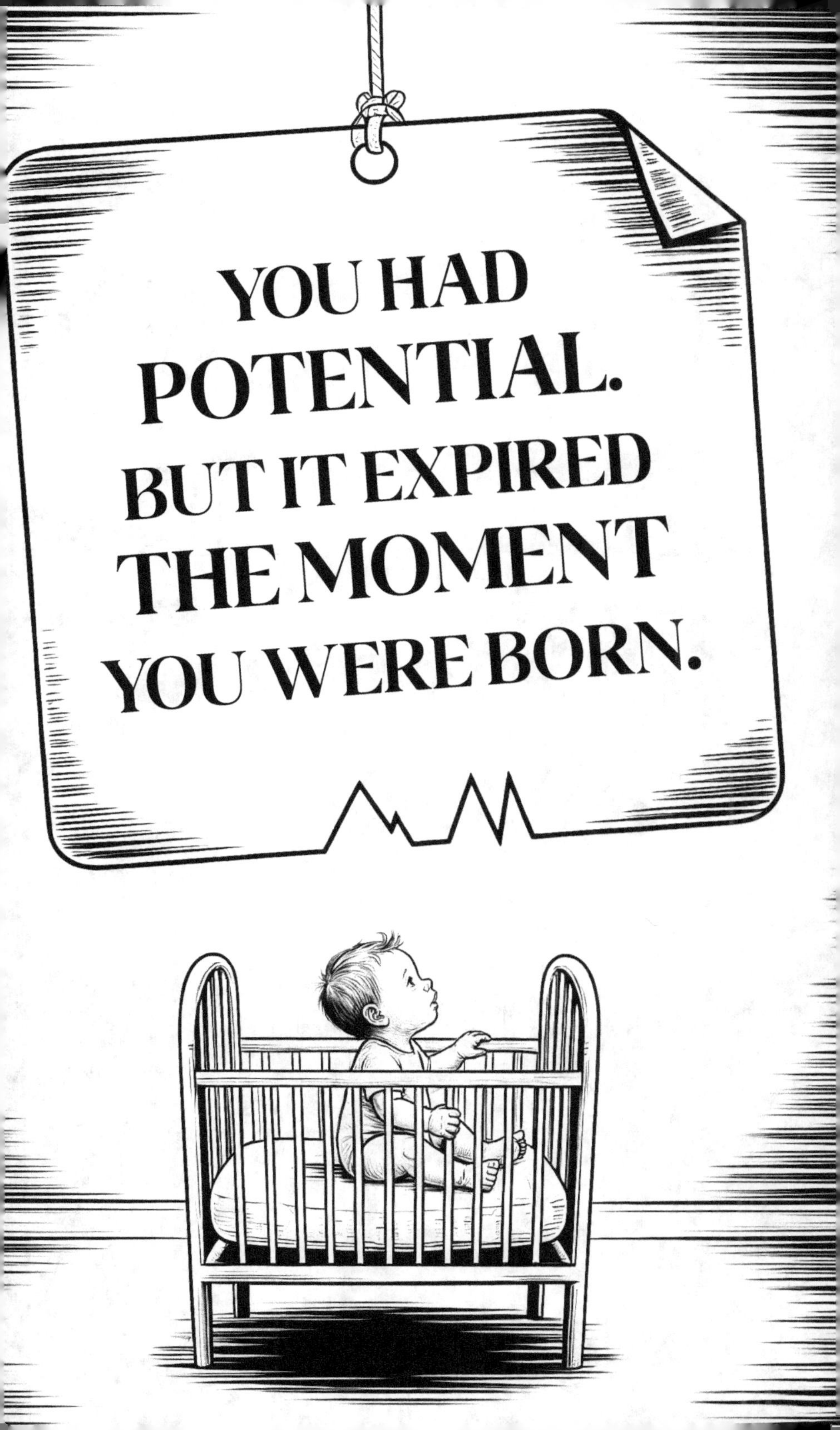
YOU HAD POTENTIAL.
BUT IT EXPIRED THE MOMENT YOU WERE BORN.

YOU'RE PROOF THAT
ROCK BOTTOM
HAS A BASEMENT.

YOUR
DREAMS
EXPIRED.
CHECK THE
DATE.

YOU'RE THE HUMAN VERSION OF A SOFTWARE BUG.

EVEN
YOUR
MISTAKES
HAVE
MISTAKES.

YOU'RE THE SEQUEL NOBODY ASKED FOR.

YOU BRING
NOTHING
TO THE TABLE...
AND THE
TABLE AGREES.

YOUR PARENTS
WERE THRILLED
YOU WERE
BORN...
MOSTLY FOR THE
TAX BENEFITS.

PROGRESS
IS SLOW.
BECAUSE YOU
NEVER
STARTED.

DESTINY
CALLED.
YOU
DECLINED.

EFFORT'S
OVERRATED.
FAILURE
IS YOUR
BRAND.

YOU'RE
THE PUNCHLINE
NOBODY
LAUGHS AT.

YOU'VE GOT
99 PROBLEMS...
AND CONGRATULATIONS,
THEY'RE MULTIPLYING.

HOPE'S ON
VACATION.
YOU WEREN'T
INVITED.

YOU'RE LIVING THE DREAM... SOMEONE ELSE'S, OBVIOUSLY.

YOU'RE PERFECTLY INCAPABLE.

CONGRATULATIONS.

YOUR REIGN OF
GLORIOUS
FAILURE
BEGINS TODAY.

CONGRATULATIONS!
YOU FINISHED
THE BOOK.
YOUR
FIRST-EVER
ACHIEVEMENT.

THE END... (UNFORTUNATELY)

You made it. Against all odds and despite your own tendency to leave things unfinished, you have reached the end of this journey. This is officially the most impressive thing you've done all week.

This book didn't fix you. It didn't spark joy. It didn't ignite your inner fire and it certainly didn't motivate you to "crush" anything. That is exactly the point.

If you ever feel dangerously close to becoming productive, or if you accidentally start seeing the glass as half-full, flip back a few pages. Let reality remind you that the glass is actually just poorly designed and likely needs washing.

Now, go. Continue being gloriously average. It suits you perfectly.

S. B. COLLECTIVE

AUTHOR'S NOTE

Well… look at you.

You actually made it to the end of this beautifully unhelpful collection. That alone is a level of follow-through we honestly didn't expect from someone like you.

Since you've proven you are capable of finishing at least one thing, we have a small, low-effort request.

If these pages made you laugh, sigh, or question your life choices, please consider leaving a review on Amazon.

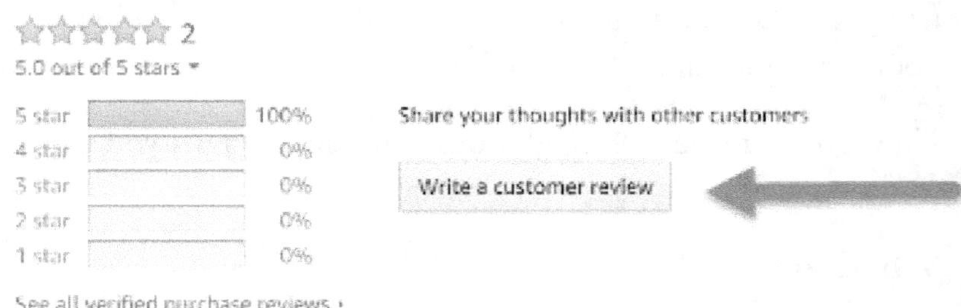

Reviews are the only thing keeping this project alive. It is a bit ironic considering the subject matter, but here we are. Your feedback helps other uninspired souls find exactly what they aren't looking for.

Go ahead. Share your thoughts, your disappointment, or your unexpected enjoyment.

S. B. COLLECTIVE

(We knew you'd finish eventually. For once.)

www.ingramcontent.com/pod-product-compliance
Lightning Source LLC
Chambersburg PA
CBHW050959050726
47592CB00007B/2635

* 9 7 8 1 7 6 4 5 1 5 0 0 9 *